Dane Love is the author of numerous books on Scottish local history. He was born in countryside near Auchinleck. He is descended from Robin Love, who fought for Bonn Prestonpans and Culloden. A member of Ayrshire Archaeological and Natural History Secretary of the Scottish Covenanter Memorials Association and a Fellow of the Socie works as a Principal Teacher at Irvine Royal Academy. In his free time, he and his wife visiting historic sites and doing research.

John Cowane's House, St Mary's Wynd.

Title Page and Back Cover: Ordnance Survey Six Inch Map of Stirling in 1896.
Following Page: Barnton Street and Maxwell Place from Murray Place.

A Look Back at
STIRLING

Dane Love

CARN PUBLISHING

© Dane Love, 2020.
First Published in Great Britain, 2020.

ISBN - 978 1 911043 11 9

Published by Carn Publishing Ltd.,
Lochnoran House,
Auchinleck,
Ayrshire, KA18 3JW.

www.carnpublishing.com

Printed by Bell & Bain Ltd.,
Glasgow, G46 7UQ.

The right of the author to be identified as the author of this work has been asserted by him in accordance with the Copyright, Designs and Patents Act, 1988.

All rights reserved. No part of this publication can be reproduced, stored, or transmitted in any form, or by any means, electronic, mechanical or photocopying, recording or otherwise, without the express written permission of the publisher.

Introduction

Stirling is one of the most historical towns or cities in Scotland (it was granted city status by Queen Elizabeth on 22 April 2002). It was the combined geography of the castle rock, the lowest crossing point on the Forth, and the location between the Highlands and Lowlands, that made it ideal as a centre of control. Thus, the kings and queens of Scotland often made it their base, and here parliament met for many years. The former parish of Stirling covered 1,935 acres, one of the smaller parishes in Scotland, and the town quickly outgrew it, spreading into St Ninians and Logie parishes. The town was created a Royal Burgh in 1119 by Alexander I, though some claim that an earlier charter had been issued by Malcolm II. The royal burgh was enlarged in 1888 to take in St Ninians, and again in 1939, subsuming Cambusbarron, Whins of Milton and Causewayhead.

Even earlier, there was probably an ancient fort on Castle Hill, and the adjoining Mote Hill contains a vitrified fort, which has been proved to date from the first to second century AD, or Roman times, perhaps being destroyed by them. The Romans passed this way, and established a fort or marching camp somewhere around Craigarnhall, three miles north-west of the castle. The main Roman Road passed by the town to the west, though older maps indicate the line of one running parallel with the road through Newhouse and St Ninians. An ancient stone overlooking Ballengeich was said to mark the spot where the Second Legion had a lookout.

Adjoining the castle, a town grew up, arranged across the leeward side of the rock on which the fortress stands. All around was either marsh or water, making the community reasonably well defended. To improve this, however, a town wall was constructed in 1547, and it is one of the few such examples in Scotland. Most of the surviving parts are on the south side of the hill, and there is much debate as to what extent, if any, a wall existed to the north side.

The history of Stirling from 1100 until 1600 mirrors that of Scotland, the town being the virtual capital of the country. With the crown based at the castle for centuries, many nobles had town houses or dwellings in the burgh, making it one of the most important communities in Scotland. Major events occurred in the vicinity, such as the Battle of Stirling Bridge, won by William Wallace's army, in

1297, and the Battle of Bannockburn, won by Robert the Bruce's men in 1314. The former is commemorated by the prominent Wallace Monument on nearby Abbey Craig (erected 1861-69 to plans by John Thomas Rochead), the latter by a statue of Bruce on his horse (sculpted in 1964 by Pilkington Jackson), located on the field of Bannockburn. Lesser battles hereabouts include that of Sauchieburn, won by Prince James over his father, King James III, in 1488. The king was buried at Cambuskenneth Abbey. The town suffered during the Jacobite risings of 1715 and 1745, after which it has enjoyed centuries of peace – even during the Second World War only two bombs landed in the town (on 20 July 1940) – one causing no damage as it fell in a field, the other destroying the spectators' stand of King's Park Football Club. Only three people had to go to hospital with minor injuries.

Stirling had a varied industrial past, with manufactories for woollens, tartan, carpets, carriages, shawls and agricultural implements. It had a nail manufacturing plant for decades and horse-drawn carriages, then buses, were manufactured in the town. To the south and east there were considerable coal fields, and the town had many miners living in it during the early twentieth century. These have gone, leaving the town surviving on tourism, the University of Stirling (established in Airthrey Castle policies in 1967) and local services. The harbour at Stirling was at one time fairly successful, with around thirty vessels using it in 1850. The largest vessel was seventy tons burden – today the only vessels on the river belong to the Stirling Rowing Club, founded in 1891. There were a number of cattle markets in the town, buying and selling sheep, cattle and other livestock from a wide hinterland, but these have been relocated to Hill of Drip and Millhall.

It was the arrival of the railway in 1848 that brought prosperity to modern Stirling. The Forth Bridge had still to be built (opened 1890), so almost every train from Edinburgh or Glasgow heading north passed through. Conversely, the trains allowed Stirling produce to be sent to larger markets more readily, and the woollen factories blossomed. A new water supply from Touch was inaugurated in 1848, and larger water mains were laid in 1908 to improve the supply. Gas lighting was introduced in 1826. Electricity arrived in the town in 1900. Larger industry arrived, such as Alexander's buses, the Grampian Motor Company, British American Tobacco's cigarette factory, Rocksil insulation works, and the University of Stirling's innovation park was created in 1986 to develop and nurture businesses with a high-growth potential.

The Stirling we see today has been influenced by this ancient history, but also by more recent developments, with new housing and industrial units surrounding the old town to the east and south. The first council houses were erected at the Shiphaugh in 1919, soon to be followed by others at St Ninians then Raploch. Eventually, the council had built over 2,000 new homes, and work could commence on the demolition of the overcrowded slums at the Top of the Town, though not without losing much of the old town's historical character. The Thistle Centre was opened in 1970, to be extended later into the Marches in 1997. East of the town centre the extensive Springkerse Industrial Estate is home to most industrial and retail employment. The M9 motorway bypassed the town to the west, opening on 28 December 1973, making the centre of the community a bit quieter, allowing the redevelopment of some streets into pedestrian-focussed areas.

Stirling Castle

Stirling owes its origins to the great rock on which the castle now stands. No doubt, long before the place was fortified by masonry, there was a prehistoric fort on top, such is its ideal location for defence. The earliest reference to a castle here dates from the twelfth century, when Alexander I endowed the chapel, and it was an important stronghold for the Scottish crown. What visitors see today has developed over the centuries, from royal stronghold, to garrison for soldiers, to major heritage attraction. The large block on the highest point in the illustration is the Palace, dating from 1540, where James V lived. On the ceiling of the King's Presence Chamber were the carved Stirling Heads, removed for almost 250 years after one fell on a soldier garrisoned here! The central courtyard is the Lion's Den, at one time home of a menagerie. The exterior walls are covered with carvings which were not always to visitors' tastes. The gable to the right is the Great Hall of 1501-3, one of the finest mediaeval halls in the country, at one time divided into floors and rooms to create billets for soldiers. Previously it was the meeting place of parliament, and in 1594 Prince Henry was baptised here. It is 125 feet in length and has been restored to its one-time magnificence. To its side is the former Mint, or Cunzie House, parts of which date from 1381, perhaps the oldest surviving masonry in the whole castle. The twin towers of the Forework gatehouse are visible to the right of this, and right again is the Guard House and site of the Elphinstone Tower. Not seen in the picture are other important buildings, such as the Chapel Royal of 1594, and the King's Old Building of the fifteenth century, restored in 1857 after a fire. It contains the regimental museum of the Argyll and Sutherland Highlanders. The castle stopped being a military depot in 1964. The large house in the woods to the left is Snowdon House, demolished around 1920 to allow the Snowdon cemetery to be laid out.

Monuments and Statues

To the left is a large and ornate memorial to Margaret Wilson, one of the Wigtown Martyrs, which is located on the shoulder of Ladies' Rock in the Mar Place Cemetery. The statue shows the martyr in the act of reading the Scriptures, with her younger sister Agnes by her side. A lamb rests at their feet, and over both is a guardian angel. The statue was erected in 1859 and was the work of Handyside Ritchie. Originally, the statue was open to the elements, but in 1867 an ornate cast iron frame and glass cupola was raised over it, making it one of the most distinctive monuments in Stirling, if not the whole of Scotland. The cupola was designed by John Thomas Rochead (1814-1878), who is better known for his design for the Wallace Monument on Abbey Craig. The frame was cast at the Sun Foundry in Glasgow, and when it was added, a marble lamb that lay at the feet of Margaret, had to be removed. The cost of the monument was financed by William Drummond, of the Drummond Tract Enterprise. Margaret Wilson was one of the Wigtown martyrs, two women who were drowned in the rising Solway Tide on 11 May 1685. They were both Covenanters, and the other martyr, Margaret MacLachlan, was a woman in her sixties. To the right is the South African war memorial, located on the castle esplanade. It was unveiled on 12 January 1907 by the Duchess of Montrose to commemorate the officers, non-commissioned officers and men of the 1st Battalion Princess Louise's regiment, or the Argyle and Sutherland Highlanders, who lost their lives in the Boer War of 1899-1902. There are 149 names listed on the bronze panels and the bronze statue was the work of W. Hubert Paton. In the distance is the stone statue to King Robert the Bruce. It was sculpted by Andrew Currie and designed by George Cruikshank. The statue was unveiled on 24 November 1877 by Lady Alexander of Westerton. It has a few metal parts, including the axe head, sword and parts of the shield.

A Look Back at STIRLING ~ *page 11*

Argyll's Lodging

Argyll's Lodging is one of the finest surviving Renaissance palaces in Scotland. When Stirling was an important centre of Scottish royalty and government, many landowners wished to have town houses here. Many of these have gone, such as Mar's Wark (which is in ruins), but others survive, such as Bruce of Auchenbowie's House, at the top of St John Street. The building we see today on Castle Wynd has been built at different periods. The oldest part is an L-shaped tower house located at the north-east corner, erected in the sixteenth century, perhaps by the Traill family, who were merchants in the town. It still has its old vaulted ground floor. This tower was extended to the west and south by Sir William Alexander of Menstrie (who was created 1st Earl of Stirling in 1633), the date 1632 and arms appearing on the entrance porch. It was Alexander who established the colony in 1621 that was to become Nova Scotia. The house has been host to numerous famous folk from the past, some welcomed in, others commandeering it. These include King Charles II in 1650, a guest of the Marquis of Argyll; King James VII (whilst Duke of Albany), in 1681, at which time he was presented with the freedom of the burgh of Stirling; the 2nd Duke of Argyll held a council of war here in 1715 during the Jacobite rising; and the Duke of Cumberland in 1746, awaiting the repair of Stirling Bridge, so that he could continue on his pursuit of the Jacobites. The house passed through a number of hands in the eighteenth century until 1791 when it was purchased by the Crown and converted into a military hospital, there being a lack of space at the castle hospital. In October 1893 Sergeant Seymour Basket, keeper of the hospital, committed suicide there by swallowing excess morphine. The hospital closed in 1964 and the building was used as a youth hostel from then until 1993, after which it was restored to how it would have looked in 1680, and opened to the public as a heritage attraction.

Mar's Wark

The ruined façade of Mar's Wark, as it is commonly known today, is located at the top end of Broad Street. The walls were part of the Earl of Mar's Lodging, another elaborate town house, similar to Argyll's Lodging. The building was erected around 1570-72 as a fine Renaissance mansion for John Erskine, 6th Earl of Mar. Tradition claims that some of the stone was taken from Cambuskenneth Abbey, and within the ruins the remains of a cross can be seen. There is an old story that relates how the building became cursed as a result of the plunder of the abbey, and that the family were never to enjoy its planned luxuries. The Erskines were appointed as Hereditary Governors of Stirling Castle by King David in 1360 and in 1562 became Earls of Mar. Perhaps to show off his new title, Mar's Wark was started a few years later. Along the side of the street are a series of doorways and small windows, reckoned to have been little shops, looking onto the town's main marketplace. On the finely hewn stonework of the wall is a string course, marking the upper rooms, where there were larger windows. Two semi-octagonal towers project to either side of an arched pend, over which is the royal coat of arms. The building was still unfinished when the town was attacked by the followers of Mary Queen of Scots on 3 September 1571 and Mar used it as a safe place for residents to shoot at Huntly and Hamilton's party. The 11th Earl stayed in the building in 1715. In 1733 it was leased by the town council for £30 Scots per annum and they converted it into a workhouse. When the Jacobites attacked the castle in 1746, the lodging was seriously damaged. In 1782 the council proposed taking the building down, which was accordingly done, apart from the decorative façade. Whether this was kept for ornamental reasons or whether, as some say, it was kept as protection against the north-west winds, is unknown. It is preserved as an ancient monument.

A Look Back at STIRLING ~ page 15

Church of the Holy Rude

Located at the top of Broad Street, the Church of the Holy Rude is distinguished by the fact that it is only one of two surviving churches in Britain that have held a coronation – the other being Westminster Abbey in London. It was here, in Stirling, that the infant King James VI was crowned on 29 July 1567. The preacher on that occasion was Rev John Knox, the great reformer. The church has a much older history, however, for it occupies the site of a place of worship of 1129. The present structure was started in 1456, the western nave and tower originally being of that date. Stirling had suffered destruction by fire in 1452 and the Douglases destroyed parts of the town in 1455. The nave has an important mediaeval timber roof and vaulted aisles. The eastern choir dates from 1507. John Knox preached in the church again in 1559, just as the Reformation was kicking in. In 1651, when General Monck was attacking Stirling Castle, he used the church tower to fire at the castle's defences. In retaliation, occupants of the castle shot back, and marks made by musket balls survive on the church tower. Around 1656 the church was divided by a wall across the nave, creating the West and East churches. This occurred due to a dispute with the minister, Rev James Guthrie, and the council. Guthrie was later to be hanged in Edinburgh, the first Presbyterian minister in Scotland to suffer execution. Restoration work took place in 1803, 1818 and 1936-40, when the congregations united and the dividing wall was removed and the transepts extended. The entrance is through one of these new transepts, centrally placed in the illustration. Immediately behind it, the size of the pillars at the crossing indicate that there were plans to have a tall tower here. In the nineteenth and twentieth century the church has had new stained glass inserted into the windows. The organ, by Rushworth & Draper, is the largest romantic organ in Scotland. Also inside is a memorial to Alexander Durham, purse bearer to Mary, Queen of Scots, and James VI.

A Look Back at STIRLING ~ *page 17*

Cowane's Hospital

Hidden to some extent by the Church of the Holy Rude is John Cowane's Hospital. This was built in 1637-48 and was designed by John Mylne, the royal master mason. John Cowane (1570-1633) gifted 40,000 merks for the erection of a hospital for 'sustenying therintill the number of tuelf decayed gildbroer, burgessis and induellars'. However, in its early years, many of the guild members refused to admit to being decayed! When Daniel Defoe visited Stirling in 1723, he described the building as 'a very good hospital'. Cowane was a local merchant, ship-owner and money-lender. Some also say that he was involved in piracy. He became a member of the Scottish parliament, and though he never married, he had at least one illegitimate son. The kirk session of the Church of the Holy Rude fined him £6 for this misdemeanour. E-shaped in plan, the entrance to the building is located through the base of the bell tower, on which is a statue of Cowane himself, known locally as 'Auld Staneybreeks'. Locals used to claim that he jumped down from this position at midnight on Hogmanay to dance in the yard, but that over time the bells above made him deaf. In 1852 the building was reconfigured – the floor of the taller rear block being removed to create a large guildhall, lit by the tall windows. The building was later used as a schoolhouse and a hospital during epidemics. To the east of the building is the walled garden, originally laid out in the 1660s, but redesigned in 1712 by Thomas Harlaw, gardener to the 6th Earl of Mar. He added the bowling green, which was used by many years by the Guildhall Bowling Club. However, the size of the green didn't match the regulations for many years. In the adjoining parterre is an old sundial, originally erected in 1673, but which had been rebuilt in 1727. Cowane's Hospital Trust still exists, now Scotland's second-oldest surviving charitable trust, giving special housing to those in need. The building was restored in the twenty-first century and is still used for concerts and meetings.

A Look Back at STIRLING ~ *page 19*

Broad Street Looking East

An old view of the top end of Broad Street, as seen from the roof of the Church of the Holy Rude. This is the narrow end of the street, the broad market place, with market cross, being located at the bottom end. On the left of the image is Argyll's Lodging. The double storey building in the centre foreground is Mar Place House, currently Hermann's Restaurant. In 1889 the owner, Councillor William Cunningham, sued the *Stirling Observer* for slander, the paper having printed a series of anonymous letters defaming him. The tall white building next door dates from the early eighteenth century, an arched pend leading through to the back court. Next door, the three-storey building is perhaps older, the central pend leading to the back gardens, where there was an observatory, the pointed roof of which is just visible in the picture, abutting Mar Place House's right-hand chimney. The site of this is now part of Kelly Court sheltered housing, erected in 1984. The next building down has a wide pend, leading to Banks' Court. The white building with the double-gable facing the street is Graham of Panholes' Lodging, an old building restored in 1958-59 by Walter Gillespie. The ground floor was vaulted, the pedimented door being modern. In the courtyard is a square turnpike stair. The long back-rigg wing has been demolished. It is said the house belonged in 1529 to James Kirk, Commissioner to the Earl of Argyll. It passed to John Graham of Baldoran, town clerk, and to his son, William Graham of Panholes. Next door, the single white gable facing the street, belongs to James Norie's Lodging. This was erected in 1671 for Norie, town clerk in Stirling. The façade has pediments over the windows, bearing dates and mottoes. At the top of the gable is a carved head, claimed to be of Norie wearing his wig. The house is tall but narrow to the street, a result of the taxation payable on frontages. Again, it was rebuilt in 1958. In the distance Queenshaugh is seen still with some open fields.

Broad Street and Tolbooth

Broad Street was Stirling's original marketplace, hence the wide street which had narrower entrances and exits. This view is looking up towards Mar's Wark and shows the street prior to the redevelopment of the 1950s. Many buildings have been replaced, but some individual ones survive. On the right edge was Michael Conroy's general store. The gabled building with the rubble outside was Edward Welsh's provisions store. Next was David Brock's Ye Auld Mercat Cross pub and wine merchants. He took over from George Philips in 1896. The darker coloured house next door was Sir John Dinely's House – he advertised for a wife in 1788! Between it and Brock's was the Reformed Close, which led to St Mary's Wynd. On the left-hand edge of the picture was Catherine Darmody's warehouse. The large four-storey building was Provost Wright's – he sold almost everything and was a successful businessman. Through the pend and up a stair was Stirling School of Art's library and museum. The lower white building was Broad Street Brewery, where James Burden produced ale and porter. All of these buildings have gone. The next building, complete with the tower, is Stirling's Tolbooth, which survives, having been converted into a venue in 2001. The building dates from 1703-5, being designed by Sir William Bruce, with additions of 1785. On 13-14 July 1820 John Baird and Andrew Hardie were tried here for their rebellion at Bonnymuir. Found guilty, they were executed in the street in front on 8 September, however, the Stirling hangman refused to carry this out, and it was done by a Glasgow medical student. Today, they are regarded as political martyrs. Visible in the street is the town's market cross. The old cross was removed in 1792, as it hindered traffic flow, with only the carved head surviving. On 23 May 1891 a new cross was unveiled at the instigation of Provost Robert Yellowlees, onto which the old unicorn was affixed. Many of the 1930s and 1950s buildings in Broad Street have been designed by Sir Frank Mears, often incorporating old stones rescued from earlier structures.

A Look Back at STIRLING ~ page 23

Darnley's House

Darnley's House is a tower house that dates from the late sixteenth century, one of the finest in Stirling. It has a vaulted ground floor, now occupied by the Darnley coffee house, and originally the upper floors were reached by a spiral stairway located in the re-entrant angle to the rear, accessed through an arched pend to what was known as Graham's Court. Thus, the ground floor and upper floors were unconnected. Plaques on the wall tell of the tradition that this was the infant nursery of Prince James, later King James VI, and his son, Prince Henry, and that Henry Stewart, Lord Darnley, stayed here in 1565 when Prince James was baptised. What is known is that the house became the property of Sir Alexander Erskine of Gogar, who died in 1592, then his son, Thomas, who was created Earl of Kellie in 1603, and then his descendants, the Earls of Mar. In the mid seventeenth century the building was occupied as an inn by Janet Kilbowie, often used by the provost and baillies of the town for special events. On 7 August 1651 the council of Stirling surrendered to General George Monck within Kilbowie's inn. In later years the house was subdivided, in the early nineteenth century the first floor becoming a branch of the Bank of Scotland. When the bank moved to new premises down the town, the building became the offices of the Sheriff Clerk. The ground floor was divided into two shops – occupied since at least the 1860s by Alexander Henderson, bookseller and stationer, and the Bow Street Dairy, proprietrix Jean Calder in the 1880s. Whilst the building was boarded up, awaiting restoration, the roof was damaged by fire in 1946. The house was originally to be demolished as part of the redevelopment of the Top of the Town in 1951, but when bulldozers started, they found the structure to be far more solid than expected. Locals stepped in quickly to save the building, and it was redeveloped into flats in 1957, seen here with the scaffold, the date and Erskine arms carved in stone over the pend.

A Look Back at STIRLING ~ page 25

The Bow

This picture shows Bow Street when it had virtually been demolished by the council as part of its plans to clear away the slums at the Top of the Town. The photographer is standing at the ramp where the Broad Steps used to be, adjoining St John Street, looking north to the foot of Broad Street. On the left is the old Baker Street Post Office with James Neil's butcher's shop next door. The post office had for many years been the premises of various watchmakers. The gap site was where the Blue Bell Inn, renamed Globe Tavern, then the Super Fish Restaurant was. To the right were the buildings of upper Baker Street. The large open gable is that of Darnley House. A new gable had to be erected to close off the building when it was restored, and the upper parts of the front wall, dormer windows and roof were rebuilt. The large wing to the rear was partially demolished and rebuilt. The building to the right with the ivy is Moir of Leckie's House, which was also saved. This house was erected in 1659 for David Moir of Leckie, who probably bought the property that stood there from the Stirlings of Keir. It is L-planned, with a vaulted ground floor. In the early eighteenth century two Venetian windows were inserted into the building on the east side, originally looking over the house's gardens, but today over the adjoining park. The house was restored as three flats in 1957-58. Instrumental in saving some of Stirling's old buildings was the Thistle Property Trust, which was founded in 1928 with the intention of renovating some of the historical old properties into modern homes. The trust saved a number of buildings, but the council was keen to redevelop, buying out the trust in 1952 and replacing some trust properties and surrounding slums with new buildings, often designed with a Scots-style architecture. Thus, the area to the right, where the digger and lorry is, was rebuilt with flats, designed by Sir Frank Mears, but executed by Walter H. Gillespie, Stirling's burgh architect.

Old Buildings

Stirling had many traditional Scots-style buildings prior to a general clearing away of them in the 1930s-50s. Others were removed even earlier, such as the pawn shop shown to the left. This was located at the top of Baker Street, on the corner with Bow Street, backing onto Spittal Street. Locally, this building was referred to as The Mint, for it was reckoned that it was here that the Scottish coinage was struck. At an earlier date the mint was located within the castle, and a building outside the Great Hall is often referred to as The Mint. In the fifteenth century there is reference to an Alexander Tod, 'moneyer to His Majesty', maker of gold and silver coins. Where this was done is not known, but may have been in this building. The term 'bawbee' may have originated in Stirling, for copper coins were minted here, using copper mined at Airthrey. Initially they were referred to as 'babies' and 'half babies'. In 1858 the Wallace Tavern occupied the building but it was demolished in 1871 to improve traffic flow at the Top of the Town, the distinctive Broad Stairs being removed to create a ramp from Spittal Street to Bow Street. The picture on the right is of the Hangman's House, located in St John Street. Historically, the burgh hangman was supplied with a free house, clothing and a weekly allowance. There were some downfalls, however, for should he depart the confines of the town without obtaining prior leave, then this was a capital offence. In Stirling the hangman appears to have been known as the 'staffman', perhaps indicating that he carried a staff at official events. The hangman wasn't only to carry out executions, of which there weren't that many, but also to administer corporal punishments to wrongdoers, including brandings and whippings. The Hangman's House was located adjacent to the old justiciary buildings and was a traditional old Scots building, with corbie-stepped gables. To the right, on looking at the front from the street, an exterior stair led up to the first floor, where the house was.

A Look Back at STIRLING ~ *page 29*

High School

What is now the Stirling Highland Hotel was built in 1854-56 as the new Stirling High School. A massive gothic building, the architects chosen were J., W. H. and J. M. Hay of Liverpool. The foundation stone was laid on 3 August 1854 by Sir A. C. Maitland of Sauchieburn, and the original building was that part to the right of the bell tower. When it opened there were various masters, including James Donaldson (1831-1915) in charge of classics. He charged seven shillings and sixpence per quarter. He was to become Professor Sir James Donaldson, Principal of St Andrews University, and was knighted in 1907. Another noted rector was Andrew F. Hutchison (1838-1903) who was appointed at the age of 28 and who remained for around thirty years. This view shows the original main front, facing Academy Street, the entrance to the courtyard being through an archway in the tower sporting the clocks. On the tower is a sculpture of children, the work of Handyside Ritchie. On the extreme left of the image one can make out the dome of the observatory. This was sponsored by Sir Henry Campbell-Bannerman and added when the high school was extended further down Spittal Street. Inside there is still a 130-year-old Newtonian telescope. The extension was added in 1887-90, to plans by James MacLaren. Another early extension was built over the site of the old Trades Hall and the former South Free Church was also incorporated. In 1945 there had been plans to relocate the school, due to its cramped site, but the education offices and a new extension were used to keep it open. However, an increasing roll, around 1,100 by 1962, meant that the school needed to relocate and it was closed when a new building was opened at Torbrex – the teachers and pupils marched from the old school to the new one on 25 April 1962. The building was then used as council offices, but in 1990-1 it was converted into a 76-bedroom hotel, new bedroom accommodation being added. Within, elements of the school were retained, such as the Headmaster's Study bar.

Erskine Church

Although locally referred to as 'the Back Raw Kirk', the Erskine Church is named from Rev Ebenezer Erskine (1680-1754), founder of the Secession Church. Erskine was minister of the West Church (in Holy Rude) from 1731, but disagreed with the Patronage Act and eventually left the Church of Scotland, or seceded, in 1733 and consequently the new denomination he formed became known as the Secession Church. With no place of worship, the new congregation were granted the use of one of Stirling's magistrate's orchards. The first place of worship for the congregation in Stirling was originally located in front of the church shown, erected around 1742, and it was within it that Erskine himself was buried. This was a cruciform-shaped building. In 1746 Erskine headed two companies of his congregation against the Jacobite rebels who threatened the town. When the church shown was erected in 1824-6, designed by Allan Johnstone, the old church was demolished. As Erskine was still buried there, the Erskine Monument was erected over his grave at a cost of around £1,000 and was unveiled on 6 December 1859. The memorial was designed by Peddie & Kinnear. A statue of Erskine can also be seen in the Valley Cemetery, sculpted by Handyside Ritchie in 1858. In the United States the Associate Reformed Presbyterian Church continues, and the Erskine Theological Seminary in South Carolina bears his name. Along the north-west wall of the churchyard were other burials, backing onto the prison wall. The 1824 building was noted for its excellent acoustics, there being a curved gallery and tiered seating. In total, there were seats for 1,450 within it. The Secession church became the United Presbyterian Church, then United Free, and eventually became a Church of Scotland congregation in 1929. In 1934 the church merged with St Mary's Mission Church, becoming Erskine Marykirk Parish Church. The church was closed in 1968, and lying empty suffered a fire in 1980. The main part of the church was subsequently demolished, and behind the classical façade a new building was erected in 1992, opening as the Stirling Youth Hostel.

Baker Street

The author of *A New Description of the Town and Castle of Stirling* (1836), is rather scathing of Baker Street, claiming it, 'has little to recommend it in point of show. The declivity is unavoidably great, and, especially towards the top, like all streets of the olden time, it is inconveniently narrow. It has, thanks to the consideration of our successive civic rulers, underwent in the course of time, a most praiseworthy renovation; for but a few generations back, the dwelling-houses projected so far over the shops, that it is said two friends on opposite sides of the street could shake hands with each other from their respective windows.' On the far right of the picture is the former Caledonian Vaults inn, which survives today as Nicky Tam's bar. It had a new hall for events added to its rear in 1874. The three buildings in the centre were some of the oldest in the street, one of them being dated 1631. The refreshment rooms was actually the Freemason's Arms, an old inn, noted for its pies and porter. It had an inscription on the façade – HEIR I FORBEARE/MY NAME OR ARMES TO FIX/LEAST I OR MYNE/SHOWLD SELL THESE STONES AND STICKS. This was added to poke fun at the owners of the Caledonian Vaults, the Craigengelts of that Ilk, who had adorned it with their coat of arms. The flat above number 25 was the birthplace of Sir John Jaffrey, 1st Baronet of Skilts (1818-1901), who became a newspaper proprietor in Birmingham and founded the Jaffray Chronic Hospital there. The middle corbie-stepped gabled building was occupied by E. Leathley's fish and fruit shop at the time of demolition. Lower down, the first gabled shop was occupied by W. Watson's boot and shoe warehouse. Upstairs was the home of Robert Stirling, a local clockmaker in the middle of the nineteenth century, whose work still exists. The three buildings were demolished and a large sandstone shop and eighteen flats were erected in 1899-1901 to plans by MacLuckie & Walker, for R. Lawson & Co. Ltd., drapers (established as a limited company in 1896).

King Street

Taken from Port Street looking uphill towards the Athenaeum, this is King Street, one of Stirling's busiest commercial streets, indeed, in 1900 there were six bank branches here. The street was at one time known as Quality Street, but it was renamed in 1820 when King George IV was crowned. First on the right is the Stirling Tract Depot building, latterly a bank, and now a restaurant named Narcissus. Over the ground floor windows were heads of Calvin, Chalmers, Guthrie, Knox, Luther, Whitefield, Wycliffe and Zwingli, now removed. The three-bayed pillared building was the Clydesdale Bank. The Golden Lion Hotel is a magnificent old building following, its slightly projecting pedimented front being distinctive. It was originally known as James Wingate's Inn, having been built on the site of Gibb's Inn, an old coaching inn where carriages to Edinburgh and Glasgow could be taken. The building dates from 1786, and was just one year old when Robert Burns visited. Other visitors include the Grand Duke Michael of Russia, who called on 8 August 1818, and Lord Cockburn in 1852. On the roadway in front of the hotel, the site of the town's New Port is marked out, one of the gates through the Town Wall. The Athenaeum building, with its curved façade and elegant spire, was erected in 1816 on the site of the old Meal Market. On the ground floor was a shop, and within, on the upper floors, were an assembly room and library. Members paid a subscription to join – those who couldn't afford the subscription could join MacFarlane's Free Library, which was located at 10 King Street until it moved to the Smith Institute in 1888. Over the projecting porch of the Athenaeum is a statue of Sir William Wallace, added in 1858 and sculpted by Handyside Ritchie. The statue was paid for by subscriptions raised by Rev Dr Charles Rogers and a sizeable donation from William Drummond. At the immediate left of the picture was Gill's Temperance Hotel, accessed by an arched doorway. No longer a hotel, it still has its Cyclists' Touring Club badge on the first-floor façade.

Stirling Co-operative Grocery

This photograph dates from 1937 and shows the interior of Stirling Co-operative Society's grocery at 14 King Street. This co-op building was erected in 1898-99 to plans drawn up by McLuckie and Walker of Stirling. It cost £10,000 to build and was opened on 4 March 1899 by the president of the society, James MacIndoe. Built with red sandstone, the building has some rather good carvings on the facade, including a scroll of text confirming that the society was 'established 1880'. The roof is adorned by two conical turrets. There appears to have been an earlier co-operative society in the town, existing from at least 1833 until 1867. The later society was founded by 49 members with a capital of £53 6s. By July 1882 it opened its first shop at 8 Craigs, by which time it had a further 100 members. Other branches include those in Barnton Street and Bow Street. There was a bakery in Cowane Street. By 1939 the society had branch shops at Causewayhead, Cambusbarron, Drip Road (1933), Fallin, Bridge of Allan and Callander. Members received a dividend on what they spent – in 1940 it was two shillings and sixpence in the pound, and non-members received less. The society also looked after its members during hard times, such as the miners' strike of 1912 when it reduced the price of bread for miners. The society also owned some domestic property, such as a block of tenement flats in Cowane Street which was destroyed by fire in August 1904. In the same year the society purchased the Royal Hotel for £6,750 and spent £10,000 changing it into new shops and offices. In 1905 it had sales of around £93,800 and in 1906 the number of members had grown to 2,793. This interior picture shows a typical shop of its time, with assistants ready to collect your goods from the shelves. A close look at the picture shows some of the goods on sale – Lothian Tea Cakes, Wrigley's P.K. gum, Epsom salts, Vaseline, Bird's custard, and Laxacon. At number 18 King Street was the society's drapery department.

Municipal Buildings

Stirling's Municipal Buildings were erected in Corn Exchange Road in 1914-18, the initial estimate of the cost being £21,000. An architectural competition was held to select a suitable design, won by J. Gaff Gillespie, of the Salmon and Gillespie partnership, in 1908. His design kept the traditional Scots baronial style, but with Edwardian overtones, confidently built in stone. By 1910 the council was still deliberating what to do, either build Gillespie's proposal, or else redevelop the buildings at the top of King Street. The First World War caused considerable disruption to the construction, indeed, only the central block and the south-west wing, seen here, were built. The foundation stone was laid on 11 July 1915 by King George V, though this was done remotely from the County Buildings in Viewforth. This was carried out by an electric wire being strung up through the streets of the town from the County Buildings. When the king pressed a button, the electricity switched on a motor at the Municipal Buildings, lowering the stone into place. Within it was placed a leaden casket, containing coins of the realm from a sovereign downwards, *The Times, Glasgow Herald, Scotsman, Stirling Observer, Stirling Sentinel, Stirling Journal*, a Stirling directory, copies of the burgh charters, and photographs of the councillors and officials. The stone for the buildings came from Blackpasture and Blaxter quarries, and as there was a war on, the masons employed were all over the military age. During construction work, Robert Taylor fell from a scaffold to his death on 27 March 1916. On the apex of the gable is a statue of Mary, Queen of Scots – other sculptures are of a soldier and minister, representing 'the country of the Cross and Sword'. There is a stained-glass window representing King Alexander II presenting the royal burgh charter to Stirling in 1226. Around 1946 part of the missing block was added to the right of the main entrance, but the final addition, at the corner of St John Street, was built in a totally different style, planned by the burgh architect, Walter H. Gillespie, and erected in 1965-8.

Stirling Library

The Stirling Public Library building was erected in 1903-4 to plans by Harry Ramsay Taylor. A competition took place for possible designs for the site, and Taylor's mix of Scots baronial, Elizabethan and Greek won. This was one of many public libraries paid for by the philanthropist, Andrew Carnegie, who laid the foundation stone. Carnegie gifted £6,000 to the town, but the estimate to build it had come in at £6,600. He duly supplied a further £1,000 and, when finished, he paid off the final £290 it had taken to complete it. Carnegie remarked that he regarded this library as the finest he had seen for £7,000. The site chosen was facing the yard of the Corn Exchange, redesigned into Corn Exchange Road in 1894, angling down to Albert Place. Previously, the ground had been occupied by the back court of the Clydesdale Bank and part of the Corn Exchange yard. The library was opened on 6 February 1904 by Hew Morrison. The contractors presented Provost James Thomson with a gold key. Within was a large lending library, the main hall of which measures 40 feet by 24 feet, with space for 15,000 books. In addition, there was a large newspaper reading room and juvenile room, plus a reference library on the first floor. The first librarian was William B. MacEwen, who was paid £80 per annum plus free house, coal and light. Stirling had a number of libraries prior to Carnegie's gift. The Athenaeum had a library within it from 1816. The MacFarlane Free Library existed in King Street from 1855 until it was moved to the Smith Institute in 1882 when it took over the Stirling Subscription Library, which had been in Murray Place. The free library was established by John MacFarlane of Coneyhill (1785-1868), a considerable benefactor in the district. Beyond the Carnegie library, the building at the corner of King Street was the Clydesdale Bank. The 1899-1900 building seen here was designed by James Thomson, replacing an older Clydesdale Bank on the same site. It had an angled corner, unlike the sweep of the present building.

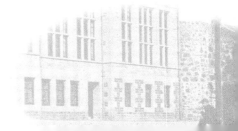

War Memorial

The war memorial in Stirling occupies a prominent site at the end of Corn Exchange Road, where it drops down to Albert Place. Other suggestions had included a triumphal arch at the entrance to King's Park, but the anticipated cost of £4,000 wasn't reached. The monument was designed by Dundee-born but Stirling-based architect, George R. Davidson (1870-1930), who won the design competition against eight other architects. Eric S. Bell (1884-1972), another Stirling architect, was second. Erected of blonde sandstone, it is topped with a bronze sculpture of two lions supporting a crown and flagstaff. On the sides are bronze plaques bearing the names of those who suffered. The memorial was unveiled on 14 October 1922 by Field Marshall Earl Haig, just after he had been presented with the freedom of the burgh in the Albert Hall. John Greig CBE, on behalf of the subscribers, handed it over to Provost McCulloch. Businesses in the town were closed for four hours whilst the ceremony took place. During the First World War, 712 men from Stirling gave their lives in battle, but their names weren't included on the monument. Instead, a book listing their names and addresses in Stirling was published. Within a short period of time, the residents were keen to have the names commemorated in bronze, and thus on 21 June 1923 two bronze panels were added. On the same day an oak shrine containing the Book of Remembrance was unveiled in the nearby library. After the Second World War, a further 211 names were added to the list of those who paid the ultimate sacrifice. The monument was restored in 2014. Many other war memorials were erected elsewhere in Stirling, such as those in the High School, Holy Rude Church, Methodist Church and Masonic Hall. In the background of the picture can be seen the junction of Glebe Avenue (behind the memorial) with Dumbarton Road (left) and Albert Place (right). The cottage in Albert Place probably dates from 1837. The building at the corner of Dumbarton Road and Glebe Road dates from around 1900.

Burns' Statue

Robert Burns is more usually associated with Ayrshire and Dumfriesshire than Stirling, but there are a few connections with him in the town. Burns visited on two occasions. In 1787 he was making a tour of the Highlands with William Nichol, master at the High School in Edinburgh, when he arrived at Stirling on Sunday 26 August. In the evening he visited the castle. During Monday he visited Barbara Hamilton at Harviestoun. On Monday evening Burns dined with Dr David Doig, rector of the grammar school, Christopher Bell, master of the English school, and Lieutenant Gabriel Forrester, from the castle garrison. Where this meal took place is unknown, but 27 August was long celebrated in the town with a Burns Supper. Burns left Stirling on Tuesday 28 August. His visit to the castle, which was mostly ruinous at the time, left him unimpressed, resulting in him inscribing some verses on a window pane at the Golden Lion Inn. These were detrimental to the royal family, describing them as 'a race outlandish'. When he was trying for a job with the excise, he realised that the lines may be used as evidence of his support for republicanism, so he returned to Stirling and broke the pane of glass. This took place on his second visit to Stirling, in October 1787. A minister known to Burns, Rev John Russell, minister in Kilmarnock, accepted a call to the West Church in Stirling in 1800, where he served until 1817. Burns knew him well in Kilmarnock, and lampooned his loud preaching. The veneration of Burns and his works has resulted in the formation of Burns' clubs across the world, and Stirling Burns Club was founded in 1891. A statue of Burns, seen in the centre of the picture, was unveiled on 23 September 1914, the event curtailed by the outbreak of war. The sculptor was Albert H. Hodge. Provost David Bayne had donated the statue and the site was gifted by the patrons of Spittal's Hospital. Naturally, the party retired to the Golden Lion for wine and cake afterwards.

Dumbarton Road

This photograph shows Dumbarton Road at the bottom of Corn Exchange Road. Dumbarton Road was originally laid out around 1790, following the line of the Town's Burn, which fed the mills, and which was culverted in 1814. By 1820 the terrace of Albert Place had been erected on the south side (behind the hedge to the right). The building on the left is the Albert Halls, which was erected in 1881-83 to plans by local architect William Simpson. There was a need for a decent-sized hall in the town, so a Public Halls Company was established in March 1881 and soon had raised over £8,000. The building has two halls – the larger of 80 feet by 67 feet, with balcony and a stage set, the latter designed by Edward L. Knapp of the Theatre Royal in Glasgow, the lesser hall being 50 feet by 29 feet. The hall was opened on Friday 5 October with a performance of Handel's *Messiah* by the Stirling Choral Society. Originally the building was referred to as 'The New Public Halls' in Albert Place, but soon the name Albert Hall was adopted. In the centre of the image is the public library, mentioned in more detail on page 43. To the right is the Allan Park Church. This was erected in 1865-67 by part of the congregation of the Erskine Church who left with the assistant minister, Rev John Gowanlock. There had been a dispute in the Erskine Church which the presbytery had tried to solve, but to no avail, eventually granting those who disagreed the right to form their own congregation. The church was designed by Peddie & Kinnear and was opened on 21 October 1867. The building had cost £5,000 to erect. Halls were added to the far side in 1933. The bell tower was reduced in height to just above the clock in 1954-5, part of a rebuild which needed strengthening to the south-east gable. The church was eventually united with St Columba's Church (Peter Memorial) on 1 April 2020 to become Stirling Park Church, this building being retained for mission work.

Glebe Crescent

This old postcard image shows Glebe Crescent, looking north towards the towers of Church of the Holy Rude and the former jail on the Castle Hill. In the Victorian period, many of Stirling's better-off merchants and dignitaries decided that they would rather live in purpose-built houses, away from the bustle of the town centre. Accordingly, the lands of Spittal's Park were developed to the south of Albert Place from 1837 onward. A formal plan was prepared in 1856. Among the streets created were Victoria Place, Abercromby Place, and Glebe Crescent. The latter was named after the glebe, or lands surrounding the manse of the local minister, whereas most of the other streets had names associated with the monarch. Glebe Crescent was built from 1879 onwards, designed by James Ronald. Ronald was a noted Stirlinger. He was a bailie with the council, but today is better known as being the author of *Landmarks of Old Stirling*, published in 1899. This book gives details on many of the burgh's old buildings. He previously published *The Earl of Mar's Lodging* in 1895. An advertisement for one of the new semi-detached villas in Glebe Crescent, built in 1880, noted that it had 'dining and drawing rooms, parlour, 4 bedrooms, bathroom, kitchen, servant's bedroom, scullery, and outhouses, and fitted up at considerable expense with all modern conveniences for the accommodation of proprietor'. Some of these early 'proprietors' included Dr Arthur W. Marchant (1850-1921), a noted composer and music teacher; his son, Lieutenant Douglas Stewart Marchant was awarded the Military Cross in 1916. Also living in Glebe Crescent was C. E. Allum, teacher of piano, organ and singing. Random events in the street included the suicide of Isabella MacDowall on 11 February 1909 at Sutherland House and the death of 68-year-old Miss Galbraith on 28 August 1935 – she had leaned too far out of the first-floor window and had fallen 23 feet to her death. 5 Glebe Crescent was used as an army hostel at the time of the Second World War. The headquarters of the Scottish Youth Hostel Association has been at 7 Glebe Crescent for many years.

Christie Memorial Clock

The Christie Memorial Clock was erected in 1905-6 in memory of Provost George Christie (1826-1902). It stands on a Corinthian column and was designed by Alexander McKenzie Lupton (1873-1945), a Stirling architect who was based in Murray Place. He also designed the Stirling Rowing Club's boathouse in 1906. The clocktower is cast in iron and was presented to Stirling Town Council in 1902 by Ellen Christie. George Christie served as provost of Stirling from 1872 until 1879. He was also the Provincial Grand Master of the Stirlingshire Masonic Lodge from 1893 until his death, hence the masonic symbolism on the stone base. In the town he was a prominent businessman, owning the Forthbank brickworks. George Street in the town was named in his honour in 1876. The street was removed with the redevelopment of the town centre, its site now Wellgreen Road. A three-quarter length portrait in oils, painted around 1870, was presented to the Smith Institute in 1907. Christie died as a result of falling down the stairs in the Midland Grand Hotel, St Pancras, London, on 19 July 1902. To the right of the image is the Black Boy Fountain, which was erected in 1849 by Robert Logan. The name refers to the small figure on the top of the structure. The cast iron fountain was manufactured at the Neilson Foundry in Glasgow, the only surviving example from that foundry. James Beaumont Neilson (1792-1865) is credited with having invented the hot blast system of iron smelting. The Neilson Foundry was more famous for casting steam locomotive parts. Some people claim that the black boy was erected to commemorate the people of Stirling who died in the Black Plague, and were buried in this locality, but this is unlikely. What is likely, however, is that this spot was used to bury plague victims, as well as those who were executed. The plague reached Stirling in 1369. The two memorials are located in the gushet of St Ninian's and King's Park roads. On the other side of St Ninian's Road can be seen one of the houses in Pitt Terrace. These date from around 1797.

Port Street

Port Street gains its name from one of the ancient gates, or ports, through the town walls, and was just named The Port on early maps. The port was originally located at the Barras Yett, where the junction with Dumbarton Road is now. On some accounts it is referred to as the South Port. This view was taken at the bottom of King Street, looking west towards Upper Craigs. The light-coloured building on the left was erected in 1928, typical of the architectural style of Burton's menswear shops everywhere, the work of their own architect, Harry Wilson. To its left was a lane leading into Orchard Place, where another port was located (the Dirt Raw Port), but this has been built over and is now an entry into the modern Thistles shopping centre. The tall tenement next door survives, a red-sandstone structure erected in 1905, the street frontage being moved back slightly to widen the road, a process commenced in 1833. Previously, the Railway and Commercial Hotel stood here. It was operated by James Grant, who in the 1850s operated a coach from there to Bridge of Allan, and trips to Balloch on the 'Forth and Clyde' – a new coach running on the new turnpike road. On the immediate right of the picture, facing King Street, is Gill's Hotel, a temperance establishment, existing from at least 1910. On the ground floor of the hotel, and turning the corner into Port Street, was Hugh Gavin and Sons' gentlemen's outfitters shop. Hugh Gavin had a draper's business in Murray Place in the 1860s, but extended here. Hugh Gavin (d. 1935) was the provost of Stirling from 1923-26. The floors above are all flats. The street here is now partially pedestrianised, and in the far part of Port Street a market is often held. Not often realised, but the Town Burn flows under the street. Originally it was used to bring water from the Park Loch to the Burgh Mill, which lay behind the buildings to the left, and which developed into the Port Mill, producing dyed woollens.

Murray Place at the Observer Corner

This view of Murray Place was taken from the end of Orchard Place, the point where Murray Place takes its dog-leg. It dates from 1939. Murray Place was named in honour of William Murray of Polmaise (1773-1847), who was a keen supporter of the town's development. The single-storey building on the right was built on part of the station's coal depot sometime around 1900. It contains the premises of Wordie & Co., general carriers and letting agents. The North Church follows, its distinctive tower being a notable Stirling landmark in its day. When it was demolished, the foundation stone was saved and incorporated in the present North Parish Church, erected at Braehead in 1971. The smaller Baptist Church follows, erected in 1854 and designed by the architect William Mackison (1833-1906). Its leaded dome and tall finial were unusual in Baptist church architecture. The white building was the Station Hotel. This part of it was a large villa that was extended to the rear around 1895, along Station Road, to form the hotel. On the far side of Station Road is the double bow-fronted County Club building, used as a business and residential base for landowning members. Next again is the tall tenement block with shops on the ground floor. On the left of the image is Birrell's sweet shop, before which it was Garner's toy shop. The premises of the Stirling Observer newspaper has a curved frontage, originally being single storey in height. The newspaper, established in 1836 by Ebenezer Johnstone, still appears weekly, outlasting other Stirling newspapers, including the *Stirling Advertiser* (1828-33), *Stirling Journal* (1820-1971) and *Stirling Sentinel* (1888-1955). The *Observer* was for many years published by Jamieson & Munro Ltd. The *Observer* only took over this shop in 1925, before which it was the bookshop of Eneas MacKay (1860-1922), who produced numerous local books and also many Gaelic ones. He came to Stirling from Inverness. The *Stirling Observer's* office was located at 40 Upper Craigs. The tall building next door, with the corbie-stepped gable facing the street, was built on the site of J. Crichton's dyeworks.

Murray Place

Murray Place links Port Street with Barnton Street, and this view is of the street looking north, towards the North Church. The street was created from 1842 onwards, previously this being open fields. In addition to creating a commercial street, removing the difficulty of needing to travel up the narrow Baker and Bow streets and then descending the steep St Mary's Wynd was one of the main reasons behind it. On the immediate right, the light building was Burton's menswear shop, actually in Port Street. The Lane led into Orchard Place, after which is the Waverley Temperance Hotel. This has been demolished and it and the lane rebuilt as an entrance to the Thistle shopping centre. At one time Stirling's post office was in the following premises, but in 1895 this moved further along the street, to a purpose-built building designed by W. W. Robertson. The County Hotel was further along the street, again a temperance establishment. The North Church, demolished in the early 1970s, was erected in 1842. The site is now occupied by bland commercial premises. The first building on the left was erected in 1862 to plans by James Hay. Originally, this was Drummond's Stirling Tract Depot, from where Peter Drummond (1799-1877) and other members of the family distributed millions of printed Christian leaflets and books. The building became too small for the business in 1877 and the enterprise moved to Dumbarton Road and only closed in 1980. The Murray Place building became a British Linen Bank then a Bank of Scotland branch. Soon after it is a pend leading to the former stables associated with the Golden Lion Hotel. At one time, the foreground street in the picture was the terminus of Stirling's tram system, opening on 27 July 1874. Initially it only had horse-drawn carriages, which hauled passengers from the town centre to Bridge of Allan for fourpence (inside) or threepence if you were willing to suffer the weather. The rails were later extended south to St Ninians. In 1913 the horses were supplemented by a petrol-powered tramcar, but by 1920 the line was closed, having lost out to buses.

Murray Place from the Post Office

This image was taken from Barnton Street looking south-east along Murray Place. The large building on the left was the post office, erected in 1895 to replace an earlier post office located elsewhere in the street. It closed in 2008. The building next door, which retained its front garden, was a branch of the Edinburgh and Glasgow Bank. It was erected in 1854 and it is claimed that it was built on the site of the Dominican Monastery, which was founded hereabouts in 1233 by Alexander II. It later became the National Bank and then the Royal Bank. The building on the right of the picture was the Royal Hotel, turning the corner into Friars' Street, originally Friars' Wynd. On the opposite corner is the Commercial Bank building, erected in 1872. Previously the Eagle Hotel occupied this corner. The light-coloured building was the Independent Congregational Church, erected in 1842, with seating for 400. The spire belongs to the North Free Church, a splendid building erected in 1851-53 by the congregation who left the North Church at the Disruption in 1843. It was designed by the Liverpool firm of J., W. H. and J. M. Hay, who also did other work in the town for the Drummond family. Internally, the church had seating for 1,200 worshippers. It became the South Church in 1902, but was closed in 1971, when the congregation merged with the Allan Park congregation, forming the Allan Park South Parish Church. The building was taken over by Stirling Baptist Church in 1989, and they remain there today. The arch-windowed factory at the end of the street was the motor and carriage works of George Thomson (established in 1805). George's grandson, James Thomson, served as provost of the town from 1900-09. Although the company made motor cars to order, they couldn't keep up and in 1921 the building seen was converted to the Olympia Picture Hall, the previous cinema burning down that year. On the centre of the roadway can be seen the horse-drawn tramlines, an actual tram being hauled along in the centre of the picture.

A Look Back at STIRLING ~ *page 61*

Railway Station

Stirling was connected to the national railway network on 1 March 1848 when the Scottish Central Railway was opened from the town to the Glasgow to Edinburgh line at Castlecary. A station was established at the east end of the town, on land that had been part of Forthside House's grounds. The work had taken three years to complete, much of it by incoming navvies, many of which drank their wages, causing major issues in the town. The line was continued north, reaching Perth on 22 May 1848. Additional lines were added – the Dunfermline line on 1 July 1852 and the Forth and Clyde Railway to Buchlyvie on 18 March 1856. The original station buildings facing onto Station Road were somewhat like a crow-stepped cottage, to which wings had been added over the years. It was designed by Andrew Heiton Jr. It was soon to prove to be too small, so in 1913-15 the new buildings were erected to the plans of James Miller, with input from W. A. Paterson, engineer-in-chief of the Caledonian Railway. This was similar in style to the previous buildings, but larger, with curved facades internally and glass roofs. On the blond sandstone gables facing the street were shields bearing CR (indicating Caledonian Railway),

1913, and the royal arms of Scotland. Between the passenger station and the gas works was a goods station, with numerous sidings and turntables. North of Forth Place and west of Forth Street was an engineering depot with large engine sheds and numerous sidings. After 1865 the railway was operated by the Caledonian Railway. Behind are the platforms, but the glazed roofs and curved walls make the station concourse one of the finest in Scotland. To catch the tourists arriving at the station, the Station Hotel was erected, extending a large villa back from Murray Place down the east side of Station Road. The Dunfermline line was closed in 1968 but was reopened as far as Alloa, for commuter traffic, in 2008. The Balloch and Callander line closed to passengers in 1934 and to freight in 1942.

A Look Back at STIRLING ~ *page 63*

Railway Engine Shed

Not so long ago, the railway line through Stirling, from Kerse Road to the railway bridge across the Forth, was bounded by various sidings and lies, with service areas, engine sheds, and storage yards. At Springbank Place, which was located under the present B&M store in Kerse Road, was a series of sidings, a turntable and an engine shed. Between the gas works and the station buildings was a large shed that originally served as the goods station. Between it and Murray Place were various sidings, small turntables in order to allow engines to be sent along lines at right angles to the one in which they arrived, and a number of bays for storing coal, much used at a time of steam locomotion. East of the railway station were numerous more sidings and sheds. One of these has been retained and, known as 'The Engine Shed', is now a training and education centre used by Historic Scotland. The building was erected between 1896 and 1913 as a goods transfer station as part of the military complex that occupied the 'far side' of the railway. The military stores depot covered all of Scotland and was established in 1892, taking over Forthside House and grounds. South of Shore Road were large carriage sheds, where work could be carried out on repairing and servicing the carriages. Between Forth Street and Wallace Street, east of the auction market, were considerably more sidings, engine maintenance sheds and a coal depot. Most of the site is now occupied by the ten-pin bowling and indoor carpet bowling alleys. More railway works extended north to the river, with sheds located in the gushet between the Dunblane and Forth and Clyde Junction Railway, now the site of the Forth Valley health board and ambulance depot. This photograph dated 1954 is of the yard adjoining Forth Street, the houses of which can be seen in the background. These have been replaced with three-storey flats forming Oliphant Court. In the shed door is a Morris Minor. The site of this shed is now the rear car park for the indoor bowling club.

A Look Back at STIRLING ~ *page 65*

Barnton Street

A continuation of Murray Place, Barnton Street heads for Stirling Bridge. Virtually every building in this old postcard of the 1950s survives, and they date from the 1880s onwards. Previously, the site of most of the buildings on the left were gardens and orchards, including Sauchie Orchard. On the left of the picture is one of Stirling Co-operative Society's branches. The society was founded in 1880 and had branches throughout the town – at King Street, Broad Street, Cowane Street, Upper Craigs and elsewhere at different times. This branch was created in 1905-6. The upper floors of the building were occupied by the Royal Hotel, built in 1840, which claimed was 'patronised by royalty'. It had 26 bedrooms and stabling for two dozen horses. On the right, Maxwell Place heads for the Shore, and the tall building in the gushet was erected 1879-80 by D. & J. MacEwen, Stirling's largest grocers and wine merchants, which was established in 1804. They had shop premises on the ground floor. It is difficult to imagine it, but at one time the Trinity Episcopal Church was located here. The first chapel was built in 1794-5 at a cost of £597 5s 0d, on land known as Friars Carse, gifted to the church by Dr Walter Stirling. It was demolished when a new church was erected on the same site in 1845, with seats for 500. This in turn was replaced by the present church in Albert Place, erected in 1878. On the ground floor of the gushet building was a newsagent and tobacconist, W. Somerville being the proprietor at the beginning of the twentieth century. In Maxwell Place can be seen the premises of John Skinner, and John Adam & Sons (established in 1934 as a grocer and merchants). On 5 October 1886 a horse pulling a milk cart bolted from the door of a dairy in Maxwell Place. It headed down Shore Road and leaped the railway gate at the level crossing, a height of five feet, pulling the cart with it. Neither horse nor cart suffered much damage!

Abbey Road

Abbey Road is located in the Shore part of Stirling, near to the River Forth. It gains its name as it aims towards Cambuskenneth Abbey, located on the opposite side of the river. At the end of the street was a passenger ferry across the water, taking locals and tourists from the town to the abbey ruins, burial place of King James III, killed at the Battle of Sauchieburn. The ferry was operated by Cowane's Trustees from 1709 until 1935, when it was replaced by the Cambuskenneth Footbridge. The terrace dates from before 1913, built in three phases from Meadow Place westwards. The nearer block of houses date from post 1896, the farther stretch from before that date. The houses were built on the site of timber yards. On the opposite side of the street, and not so photogenic, were a series of commercial and industrial premises, including four or five large timber yards and saw mills. Other businesses included the Abbeyroad Chemical Works, Forthbank Chemical Works, and a shipyard. Shipbuilding in Stirling was always troubled by the depth and shape of the Forth. Nevertheless, for a short time, Stirling held the record for having the largest ship launched. James Johnstone's business peaked in the 1850s. In 1846 he was building 90-ton, 69-feet long schooners, but by 1852 the *Stirling* was launched, a 500-ton clipper. In 1856 the *William Mitchell* was slipped into the Forth, a 1,000-ton vessel. After this the business went into quick decline and in 1859 the creditors of the business had to meet in the Golden Lion to discuss their losses. At the end of the street was the Abbey Mill, which produced woollens, cotton, and was latterly the large Stirling Steam Laundry. By the time of the Second World War, the sites were occupied by the Forth Cooperage and Abbey Road Linoleum Works, operated by Stirling Floorcloth Co. Ltd. The latter company was founded in 1919. The site of the industrial premises is now occupied by various blocks of flats, with addresses named after some of the old businesses, such as Cooperage Quay and Abbey Mill.

Stirling Territorial School

This old school photograph dates from 1915 and depicts a class at Stirling Territorial School, complete with their teacher and some random props. Originally it was erected at a site in Cowane Street by Stirling Free North Church as the Stirling Territorial Mission School. The building cost around £950, much of the funds having to be defrayed by a bazaar held in September 1866. It was adopted by the local school board under the Scottish Education Act of 1872. The building remained the property of the church, but was a financial strain on the congregation. It was sold to the school board in the early 1880s. In 1884 the school had a roll of 230 and received a grant of £192 12s 0d. In 1884 the school was considerably enlarged by the school board. When the school was closed the pupils were transferred to Riverside Primary School. In 1974 it was converted into the Cowane Centre, a theatrical and craft-based location for workshops. There have been a fair number of other schools in Stirling over the centuries. Among the longer-established ones we have Allan's School, founded in 1741 but moving to Spittal Street in 1797. The present building was erected in 1890 and remains in use today. Also in Spittal Street was the Ragged and Industrial School, opened in 1856 and now the Snowdon School. The Craigs School was opened in 1872 in George Street, the building being demolished in 1973. The Grammar School is known to have existed as early as 1150, developing over the years to become Stirling High School. Over the period, it occupied the building in Castlehill now known as The Portcullis Hotel (erected as a school in 1783). More recent schools include Riverside Primary School (opened in 1926), Raploch Primary School (opened in 1935 and moved to the Raploch Campus in 2008), Coxithill Primary School (opened in 1957), Braehead Primary School (opened in 1972), and Our Lady's R. C. Primary School (opened in 2008 to replace St Mary's). St Modan's R. C. Secondary School was opened in Barnsdale Road in 1933, moving to Royal Stuart Way in 2008.

Spittalmyre Bowling Club

Stirling had around half a dozen bowling clubs, but in recent years some of these have closed. Still going strong is Spittalmyre Bowling Club, which is hidden in the triangle formed by Wallace, Union and Bruce streets, with access from the latter. Proposals for a bowling green on Spittal's property were initially made by James F. MacIntosh (provost from 1932-35) in the late 1800s, but an appeal for funds was unsuccessful. He then formed a limited company with £1 shares. Mr James Brown Richardson of Pitgorno (1837-1902) bought 25, and then Sir Henry Campbell Bannerman bought 25. Over two years 150 shares were sold. The ground was obtained on a long lease, but it was covered in 'mire and dirt' from which it gained its name. The green and clubhouse were opened in May 1901, with £150 debt. However, this was paid off within five years. Stirling has a long association with lawn bowls. The oldest green known was laid out at the Guildhall in 1714. In 1836 the old Stirling Bowling Club was founded but it later took the name Guildhall Bowling Club. However, by the 1850s, much of the grass had sunk, leaving an uneven surface, and the old club that played there had to use the green at Bridge of Allan. In 1854 the green was re-laid, and the Stirling Bowling Club was formed. The club opened a new bowling green at Albert Place on 3 July 1858. The gothic-styled clubhouse there was erected in 1866 to plans by William Simpson. The Riverside Bowling Club has its green at the neck point in a huge meander of the River Forth at Queenshaugh. It was founded in 1921. Bowling clubs that have folded include the Guildhall Bowling Club, which played on the green at the Guildhall. It was established in 1903 and closed in 1996. The Livilands Bowling Club was founded in 1910 within the grounds of Westerlands House. It moved to the end of Randolph Crescent to allow an extension to the Royal Infirmary, but closed in 2019. The Stirling Miners' Welfare Bowling Club existed up until 1974.

Bridge Street from Mote Hill

This old image shows Lower Bridge Street to the left, with Upper Bridge Street climbing to the right. In front centre is Cowane Street. The picture was taken from the Mote Hill, where the Beheading Stone is located. The Mote Hill was thought to have been an ancient motte, or defensive structure, and evidence of vitrification has been found here. The Beheading Stone was traditionally the spot where various notables were executed, including the Duke of Albany (1425), Earl of Lennox (1425), Sir Robert Graham (1437) and Robert Menteith (1525). To the right of the image are the slopes of Gowan Hill, an eminence that is subsidiary to the Castle Hill, but which forms an open area in the centre of the present city. This open ground was attached to the King's deer park around 1500. To the left of the single-storey cottage on the immediate left of the image was the cattle market in the mid-nineteenth century. In the centre of the image was a cottage named Glencoe, accessed from Glencoe Road. To the left of centre can be seen the tower of the North Free (then United Free, then St Andrew's) Church. On the left side of Lower Bridge Street, at the end of the terrace, was a pub, John Sharp's in Victorian times, Jackie's until 2010 when it closed. Just beyond the junction with Bayne Street was another pub, but became David Bayne's grocery. It was to become the local post office by the 1890s before this was relocated farther along Cowane Street. Bayne gifted the Bridge Clock Tower in 1910. Upper Bridge Street climbs up the hillside to the right. The left-hand side of it was lined with tenements and flats, whereas the right-hand side had a number of large villas located in extensive grounds. These included Whinfield, Rosefield, Whinwell (which was a home for orphans, opened by Annie Croall in the 1890s), Comely Bank (which became Woodcliffe and then the presbytery for St Mary's R. C. Church), Marieville (where St Mary's Church was built – visible in picture), Lower Bellfield (which became a manse) and Bellfield.

A Look Back at STIRLING ~ page 75

Stirling Bridge

The name Stirling Bridge is celebrated in Scottish history as being the location of a decisive battle on 11 September 1297 between the Sir William Wallace's Scots and the much-larger English army under John de Warrene. The bridge referred to in the battle is not what is seen in this old image, but instead an older timber structure, though there is some doubt, too, that the bridge of the battle was in fact on this site. About fifty yards upstream archaeologists found the footings of a timber bridge. On 1 April 1571 gallows were erected on the bridge at the command of Regent Lennox, so that Archbishop John Hamilton could be hanged. The existing bridge had its south-western arch destroyed in December 1745 by General William Blakeney to hinder the Jacobites from reaching the main force. However, on 8 January 1746 the town surrendered to the Jacobites. The arch wasn't replaced until 1749. The bridge that survives as a footbridge, having been bypassed by the busy A9, was probably erected in the late fifteenth century at the orders of James IV. Crossing the Forth by four semi-circular arches, the bridge has triangular cutwaters, some of which are built up to form refuges for walkers to avoid traffic. The tall building at the Stirling end of the bridge, seen in the picture, was a tenement block, demolished in the 1960s. It occupied the site of a double-storey house, which was offered for sale in 1853, having belonged to James Mitchell, farmer at Auchtochter. No doubt, the Mitchell house was purchased by a developer who constructed the large tenement. Beyond, the buildings of Lower Bridge Street can be seen. Not visible in the image, to the left of the smaller buildings in Bridge Lane, was the old Flour Mill, which had become disused by the mid nineteenth century, and the old slaughterhouses. The slaughterhouse was in 1909 relocated by the council to the opposite side of Lower Bridge Street, off Laurencecroft Road. It was erected at a cost of £5,500. The new Stirling Bridge was designed by Robert Stevenson (grandfather of Robert Louis Stevenson, of *Treasure Island* fame) and was erected in 1831-32.

Raploch

Raploch was established as a small village from 1799, the cottages of which were laid along one side of Raploch Road, from the foot of Ballengeich road to Kildean Toll, each having a lease of 999 years. This picture shows the east end of the village, with the pond on the right being the water-filled Raploch Quarry. This was worked from the early nineteenth century for its sandstone, at the time commonly used for the new housing developments at King's Park. The last stone was hewn from it in 1879, to build Ronald Place. In the 1940s the pool was filled in with the refuse from Stirling, after which it became the Quarry Park. The site of the pond is now under the ground between Stirling Fire Station, erected in 1965, and the roundabout on Raploch Road. Raploch at one time had a small school in one of the houses, replaced by Raploch Road School in 1935. At the junction with Back o' Hill Road there was also a public house. Behind the cottage in the centre of the image was a market garden. The double storey semi-detached houses immediately below the castle rock on Ballengeich Road were erected in the late nineteenth century. The gables seen are actually the rear of the houses, the fronts facing across the King's Knot towards the town centre. Along Drip Road was Fisher Row, a small housing development created in 1693 by Stirling Burgh to encourage the fishing industry on the river. The name is preserved in a current street in the Raploch housing estate, which was developed from 1927 onwards, often to rehouse residents moved from the old tenements at the Top of the Town which were being demolished. A reference to Alexander Hodge and his family at Fisher Row dates from 1821 – he and his wife had been married for seventeen years during which time they had fifteen children, eleven of which were still alive. Amongst these were four sets of twins. They were brought up 'decently and comfortably' on the husband's wages of seven shillings a week, plus grazing for one cow.

Acknowledgments

I would like to thank a few people who have kindly assisted in the preparation of this book by supplying pictures or information. They are Niall Pleace, George Rillie and Anne Whitton. The other pictures are part of the author's own collection of images, gathered over a period of time.

Dane Love
Erskine of Gogar's House,
Stirling, 2020.